Great Figures in Black History

THE TUSKEGEE AIRMEN

Theia Lake

PowerKiDS press

Published in 2024 by The Rosen Publishing Group, Inc.
2544 Clinton Street, Buffalo, NY 14224

Portions of this work were originally authored by John M. Shea and published as *The Tuskegee Airmen*. All new material in this edition was authored by Theia Lake.

Editor: Theresa Emminizer
Book Design: Rachel Rising

Photo Credits: Cover, Tuskegee airmen exiting the parachute room, Ramitelli, Italy, March 1945/Libary of Congress; Cover, pp. 1-32 Wall to wall/Shutterstock.com; pp. 1, 3, 30-32 ReVelStockArt/Shutterstock.com; p. 5 Untitled photo shows: Tuskegee airmen training, Tuskegee, Alabama/Libary of Congress; pp. 7, 9, 25 Everett Collection/Shutterstock.com; p. 8 https://en.wikipedia.org/wiki/File:Buffalo_soldiers1.jpg; p.11 https://commons.wikimedia.org/wiki/File:Two_recruits_in_a_light_tank_during_training_in_mechanized_warfare_at_Montford_Point_Camp,_NC,_04-1943_-_NARA_-_532512.jpg; p. 12 https://commons.wikimedia.org/wiki/File:President_Franklin_D._Roosevelt-1941.jpg; p. 13 First Negro Nurses Land in England/Libary of Congress; p. 14, 28 EWY Media/Shutterstock.com; p. 15 https://media.defense.gov/2008/Jan/29/2000404151/-1/-1/0/080128-F-3927S-103.JPG; p. 16 https://commons.wikimedia.org/wiki/File:Eleanor-Roosevelt-WH-Portrait.jpg; p. 17 https://commons.wikimedia.org/wiki/File:First_Lady_Eleanor_Roosevelt,_center,_is_shown_in_a_digital_image_of_a_photo_taken_with_U.S._Army_Air_Corps_Tuskegee_Airman_pilot_C._Alfred_Anderson_in_March_1941_140223-F-ZZ999-001.jpg; p. 19 Ground crew sweats in a mission/Libary of Congress; p. 20 https://commons.wikimedia.org/wiki/File:Tuskeegee_reload_P-51.jpg; p. 21 https://commons.wikimedia.org/wiki/File:Benjamin_o_davis_jr.jpg; p. 23 bdomanska/Shutterstock.com; p. 24 teven Hodel/Shutterstock.com; p. 26 cpaulfell/Shutterstock.com; p. 27 https://commons.wikimedia.org/wiki/File:Pilots_of_the_332nd_Fighter_Group.jpg; p. 29 https://commons.wikimedia.org/wiki/File:Tuskegee_Airmen_-_Circa_May_1942_to_Aug_1943.jpg.

Library of Congress Cataloging-in-Publication Data

Names: Lake, Theia, author.
Title: The Tuskegee Airmen / Theia Lake.
Description: Buffalo, New York : PowerKids Press, [2024] | Series: Great figures in Black history | Includes bibliographical references and index.
Identifiers: LCCN 2023008384 (print) | LCCN 2023008385 (ebook) | ISBN 9781642826883 (library binding) | ISBN 9781642826876 (paperback) | ISBN 9781642826890 (ebook)
Subjects: LCSH: World War, 1939-1945--Participation, African American--Juvenile literature. | African American air pilots--History--Juvenile literature. | World War, 1939-1945--Aerial operations, American--Juvenile literature. | United States. Army Air Forces. Fighter Squadron, 99th--Juvenile literature. | United States. Army Air Forces. Fighter Group, 332nd--Juvenile literature. | World War, 1939-1945--Regimental histories--United States--Juvenile literature.
Classification: LCC D810.B53 L35 2024 (print) | LCC D810.B53 (ebook) | DDC 940.54/03--dc23/eng/20230222
LC record available at https://lccn.loc.gov/2023008384
LC ebook record available at https://lccn.loc.gov/2023008385

Manufactured in the United States of America

CPSIA Compliance Information: Batch #CSPK24. For further information contact Rosen Publishing at 1-800-237-9932.

CONTENTS

Who Were They? 4
Racism at Home 6
Black Military History 8
Fascism Abroad 10
Public Law 18 12
Charles A. Anderson 14
The First Lady Visits 16
Training for the Fight 18
From Classroom to Combat 20
Pantelleria 22
Fighting in the Skies 24
Red-Tail Angels 26
Heroes to Remember 28
Glossary 30
For More Information 31
Index 32

WHO WERE THEY?

The Tuskegee Airmen were the first all-Black flying unit in the U.S. military. They flew more than 1,500 **missions**. During World War II, these men became some of the most decorated, or honored, servicemen of the Army Air Forces.

Though they fought with great skill and bravery, the Tuskegee Airmen faced **racism** and **discrimination**. But, as Tuskegee Airman Herbert Carter said: "We proved that the **antidote** to racism is excellence in performance." The Tuskegee Airmen overcame the many challenges they faced, brought down their enemies, and made progress for **civil rights** both within the U.S. military and without.

Tuskegee University

The Tuskegee Airmen were trained at the Tuskegee Army Air Field in Macon County, Alabama. Famous American educator Booker T. Washington founded Tuskegee University on July 4, 1881. The Tuskegee Airmen flight training program was brought to the institute under the leadership of Dr. Frederick D. Patterson. From 1941 to 1946, about 1,000 Black pilots, or fliers, trained at Tuskegee.

This photo shows Tuskegee Airmen in training on January 23, 1942.

RACISM AT HOME

The 14th Amendment to the U.S. Constitution, which passed in 1868, officially recognized Black American citizenship and "equal protection of the laws." However, equality was far from a reality. Racist laws and practices made it so that Black Americans were **oppressed**.

Segregation was the separation of Black and white Americans in places including schools, restaurants, parks, stores, and more. From the 1880s to the 1960s, many states had Jim Crow laws that imposed segregation.

Black Americans suffered under segregation. They had fewer freedoms, opportunities, and rights than white people. Black Americans often faced open racism, mistreatment, and **violence** in the Jim Crow South.

"Separate but Equal"

In 1896, a court case known as *Plessy v. Ferguson* concluded that racial segregation was constitutional based on the idea that segregated **facilities** and services were "separate but equal." This was untrue. Black facilities often had poorer conditions and fewer means than white facilities. The *Plessy v. Ferguson* ruling wouldn't be overturned until 1954.

This photo shows a Black teacher at a school in Georgia in 1936.

BLACK MILITARY HISTORY

Although they weren't equal citizens, Black Americans served in every conflict in the nation's history, from the American Revolution (1775–1783) onward.

During the American Civil War (1861–1865), nearly 180,000 Black men served in the Union, or northern, army. Black soldiers called Buffalo Soldiers continued to serve in conflicts out West and overseas after the war ended. The U.S. government often paid them less and poorly fed them. The military gave them poor equipment, or tools, and fewer weapons than they needed.

BUFFALO SOLDIERS

Though at first they weren't allowed to enlist, or join, close to 368,000 Black Americans served in the U.S. military during World War I.

The Black WWI soldiers pictured here in 1919 received the French medal of bravery known as the *Croix de Guerre*.

FASCISM ABROAD

World War II began on September 1, 1939. At first, many Americans saw this as a European war. But on December 7, 1941, the Japanese bombed Pearl Harbor in Hawaii. The next day, the United States went to war with Japan. In turn, Germany and Italy, Japan's allies, went to war with the United States.

After the Japanese attack on Pearl Harbor, U.S. armed forces called men and women to sign up to fight back. African Americans were eager to join but weren't given the same opportunities as whites. Despite this discrimination, Black men and women served in every military branch during World War II.

Fascism and Racism

Fascism is a far-right system of government. Led by Adolf Hitler, the fascist party called Nazis controlled Germany from 1933 to 1945. Racism was a huge part of Hitler's fascist **regime**. He claimed that Jewish people were an inferior, or lesser, race and must be wiped out. Six million Jewish people were killed during World War II.

BLACK MARINES IN A WWII TANK, 1943.

More than one million Black Americans served in the U.S. military during World War II.

PUBLIC LAW 18

During World War II, the U.S. military was segregated. Black military members were limited as to the kinds of jobs and positions they were allowed to hold. They worked and fought in segregated units, usually under the command of white officers. Blacks were often **relegated** to service positions such as kitchen workers, drivers, and laborers.

On April 3, 1939, President Franklin Delano Roosevelt (FDR) passed Public Law 18 with the goal of expanding, or growing, the Army Air Corps. Under this law, programs were set up at Black colleges to train Black servicemen for jobs in the Army Air Corps.

FRANKLIN DELANO ROOSEVELT

Black women served in the Women's Army Corps and Army Nurse Corps during World War II.

CHARLES A. ANDERSON

Charles A. Anderson is sometimes called the Father of Black Aviation, or flying. Born on February 9, 1907, in Bryn Mawr, Pennsylvania, Anderson dreamed of flying from the time he was a child. In 1929, at age 22, Anderson bought a used airplane with the help of family and friends. He used this plane to teach himself to fly! He received his official pilot license later that year.

In 1940, Tuskegee Institute President Frederick Patterson asked Anderson to be the chief flight instructor, or teacher, for the school's Civilian Pilot Training Program. Anderson agreed and chose four other Black pilots to help him. The training of the first class of pilots began at Tuskegee Institute on July 19, 1941.

TUSKEGEE INSTITUTE

Anderson came to be known as "Chief."

THE FIRST LADY VISITS

On April 19, 1941, First Lady Eleanor Roosevelt paid a visit to the Tuskegee Air Field. While there, she met Chief Anderson. Though her Secret Service guards didn't like the idea, Roosevelt asked if she could take a ride with one of the Tuskegee pilots. Anderson flew the First Lady around the skies of Alabama for over an hour.

This flight brought public attention to the Tuskegee training program and provided proof that Black pilots are as skilled as white pilots. Eleanor Roosevelt became a strong supporter of the program and encouraged her husband to advance it.

ELEANOR ROOSEVELT

Eleanor Roosevelt helped persuade her husband, President Franklin D. Roosevelt, to use the Tuskegee Airmen in combat (fighting) missions.

TRAINING FOR THE FIGHT

The pilots who wished to graduate from the advanced pilot training program had to work very hard. First, they went through eight weeks of basic training. In the classroom, the students studied **navigation**, the parts of a plane, and meteorology, which is the science of weather and the atmosphere.

Those who did well moved to Advanced Flying School at Tuskegee Army Air Field. There, they received hands-on flight instructions from Chief Anderson. The airmen trained six days a week for 18 weeks, getting up before 5 a.m. and going to bed after 10 p.m.

Air Corps Personnel

Many in the program didn't become pilots but studied to work in Air Corps support jobs. Besides pilots, Tuskegee Institute provided training for medical workers, air traffic controllers, communication specialists, **mechanics**, navigators, and bombardiers, the crew members who released bombs from aircraft.

TUSKEGEE AIRMEN GROUND CREW IN MARCH 1945

All those who completed the program, including many women, were known as Tuskegee Airmen, whether or not they flew a plane.

FROM CLASSROOM TO COMBAT

Thirteen students started in the first aviation cadet (student in training) class in July 1941. Nine months later, the first five pilots graduated from Tuskegee on March 7, 1942. Together with 400 others they made up the 99th Pursuit Squadron.

Benjamin Oliver Davis Jr. was one of the first five Tuskegee pilots. The son of the first Black general in the U.S. Army, Davis graduated from the United States Military Academy at West Point, New York, in 1936 and was the first Black person to do so in the 20th century.

Davis was chosen to lead the 99th Pursuit Squadron. In April 1943, the 99th became the first Black flying squadron to see combat.

Besides being one of the military's first Black pilots, Davis (pictured here) later became the Air Force's first Black general in 1954.

PANTELLERIA

The 99th's first action was called Operation Corkscrew. During this fight, the Allies (U.S., Britain, France, and Russia) used bombers and fighter planes to attack the island of Pantelleria, which was controlled by the Axis (Italy, Japan, and Germany). Pantelleria was in the Mediterranean Sea and blocked the Allies from reaching Italy. There were over 10,000 enemy troops on the island. Attack by sea was too risky. Instead, with help from the 99th squadron, the Allies attacked from the sky!

The 99th attacked Pantelleria and protected Allied bombers, averaging two missions a day. After three weeks of bombing, Pantelleria surrendered, or yielded.

Earning Recognition

After Operation Corkscrew, an area commander wrote to Benjamin Davis Jr.: "I wish to extend to you and the members of the squadron my heartiest congratulations for the splendid part you played in the Pantelleria show. You have met the challenge of the enemy and have come out . . . stronger qualified than ever."

The defeat of Pantelleria gave the Allies a large airfield they could use for fighting in Italy.

FIGHTING IN THE SKIES

The 99th joined the 100th, 301st, and 302nd Tuskegee fighter squadrons to form the 332nd Fighter Group. Davis was made a colonel and given command of the 332nd, which was then moved to Italy for air strikes and bombing missions.

The Allied forces also continued bombing the Axis countries in Europe. Great Britain bombed at night, while the United States bombed during the day.

Allied pilots were challenged in the air by the Luftwaffe (LOOFT-vah-fuh), the German air force. At the start of World War II, the Luftwaffe had the most dangerous fighter pilots and flew the fastest planes, including the world's first jet fighter.

An American B-17 flying over chemical and oil manufacturing in Germany.

RED-TAIL ANGELS

It was the airmen of the 332nd Fighter Group's job to escort, or guard, American bombers in their missions over Italy and Germany. The Tuskegee Airmen rarely lost a bomber. This earned them a lot of respect from the men they were protecting.

The 332nd were nicknamed the Red-Tail Angels, or the Red Tails. That's because they painted their aircraft red. The airmen wanted the bomber crews to know the 332nd were there protecting them. They also wanted the German fighters to know the Red Tails were in their airspace ready to fight!

THE P-51 MUSTANG

The P-51 Mustang

The aircraft often flown by the 332nd Fighter Group was known as the North American P-51 Mustang. This was a single-seat, single-engine fighter plane and was considered the best of its kind during World War II. The P-51 Mustang could reach speeds of about 440 miles (700 km) per hour. It had four machine guns.

Pilots of the 332nd Fighter Group in Italy, 1944.

HEROES TO REMEMBER

On March 24, 1945, the Red Tails flew to Berlin, Germany, shooting down several Luftwaffe jet fighters on the way. For their support on this mission, they were awarded a Distinguished Unit Citation. On May 7, 1945, the German army surrendered to the Allies.

The brave Tuskegee Airmen earned hard-won victories that shaped the course of the war. Their contributions, and those of other Black soldiers, couldn't be ignored. On July 26, 1948, President Harry S. Truman signed Executive Order 9981, which ended military segregation.

The Tuskegee Airmen championed the fight against both fascism and racism. Their hard work and courage led the way for civil rights achievements within the military and in civilian life.

TUSKEGEE AIRMEN NATIONAL HISTORIC SITE

TUSKEGEE AIRMEN ACCOMPLISHMENTS

- FLEW MORE THAN 1,500 MISSIONS
- FLEW 15,533 SORTIES (ATTACKS BY TROOPS IN A DEFENSIVE POSITION)
- SHOT DOWN 261 ENEMY AIRCRAFT
- WON MORE THAN 850 MEDALS
- 96 DISTINGUISHED FLYING CROSSES FOR HEROICS OR EXTRAORDINARY ACHIEVEMENT WHILE PARTICIPATING AIR COMBAT
- 8 PURPLE HEARTS FOR INDIVIDUAL WOUNDED OR KILLED WHILE SERVING IN THE MILITARY
- 3 DISTINGUISHED UNIT CITATIONS FOR COURAGE AND DETERMINATION IN COMPLETING A MISSION
- 14 BRONZE STARS FOR ACTS OF HEROISM PERFORMED IN GROUND COMBAT
- 1 CONGRESSIONAL GOLD MEDAL FOR COURAGE AND DETERMINATION IN COMPLETING A MISSION

GLOSSARY

antidote: Something that fixes or counteracts something else.

civil rights: The rights of a person.

discrimination: Unfair treatment based on factors such as a person's race, age, religion, or gender.

facilities: Buildings or services.

mechanic: Someone who works on or fixes machines.

mission: A military task or operation.

navigation: The science of getting aircraft from place to place.

oppressed: Treated cruelly or unfairly.

racism: The belief that one group or race of people is better than another group or race.

regime: The period of rule of a certain government.

relegate: To assign or put someone into a lesser place.

violence: The use of bodily force to hurt, harm, or destroy.

FOR MORE INFORMATION

Books

Doeden, Matt. *Tuskegee Airmen.* Minneapolis, MN: Lerner Publishing Group, 2019

Smith, Sherri L. *Who Were the Tuskegee Airmen?* London, UK: Penguin Young Readers Group, 2018.

Websites

National Park Service
www.nps.gov/articles/tuskegeeairmen.htm
Learn more about the history of the Tuskegee Airmen.

Tuskegee Museum
tuskegeemuseum.org
Learn about the ongoing legacy of the Tuskegee Airmen.

Publisher's note to educators and parents: Our editors have carefully reviewed these websites to ensure that they are suitable for students. Many websites change frequently, however, and we cannot guarantee that a site's future contents will continue to meet our high standards of quality and educational value. Be advised that students should be closely supervised whenever they access the internet.

INDEX

A

Anderson, Charles A. "Chief," 14, 15, 16, 17, 18

B

B-17, 25
Buffalo Soldiers, 8

C

Carter, Herbert, 4

D

Davis, Benjamin Oliver, Jr., 20, 21, 22, 24

N

99th Pursuit Squadron, 20, 21, 22, 23

P

Pantelleria, 22, 23
Patterson, Frederick D., 4, 14
P-51 Mustang, 26, 27
Public Law 18, 12

R

Red-Tail Angels, 26, 28
Roosevelt, Eleanor, 16, 17
Roosevelt, Franklin Delano (FDR), 12, 17

T

332nd Fighter Group, 24, 26, 27
Truman, Harry S., 28
Tuskegee Institute/University, 4, 14, 18

W

Washington, Booker T., 4
Women's Army Corps, 13